Living Legends

商務印書館（香港）有限公司
http://www.commercialpress.com.hk

CENGAGE
Learning

Australia • Brazil • Japan • Korea • Mexico • Singapore • Spain • United Kingdom • United States

Director of Content Development:
Anita Raducanu
Series Editor: Rob Waring
Editorial Manager: Bryan Fletcher

Associate Development Editors:
Victoria Forrester, Catherine McCue
責任編輯：冼懿穎

出版：

商務印書館（香港）有限公司
香港筲箕灣耀興道3號東匯廣場8樓

Cengage Learning
Units 808-810, 8th floor,
Tins Enterprises Centre,
777 Lai Chi Kok Road, Cheung Sha Wan,
Kowloon, Hong Kong

網址：http://www.commercialpress.com.hk

http://www.cengageasia.com

發行：香港聯合書刊物流有限公司
　　　香港新界大埔汀麗路36號中華商務
　　　印刷大廈3字樓

印刷：中華商務彩色印刷有限公司
版次：2010年3月第1版第2次印刷

ISBN: 978-962-07-1868-7

出版説明

本館一向倡導優質閱讀，近年連續推出以"Q"為標誌的優質英語學習系列(*Quality English Learning*)，其中《Black Cat 優質英語階梯閱讀》，讀者反應令人鼓舞，先後共推出超過60本。

為進一步推動閱讀，本館引入Cengage 出版之*Footprint Library*，使用*National Geographic*的圖像及語料，編成百科英語階梯閱讀系列，有別於Black Cat 古典文學閱讀，透過現代真實題材，百科英語語境能幫助讀者認識今日的世界各事各物，擴闊視野，提高認識及表達英語的能力。

本系列屬non-fiction (非虛構故事類)讀本，結合閱讀、視像和聽力三種學習功能，是一套三合一多媒介讀本，每本書的英文文章以headwords寫成，headwords 選收自以下數據庫的語料：*Collins Cobuild The Bank of English*、*British National Corpus* 及 *BYU Corpus of American English* 等，並配上精彩照片，另加一張video/audio 兩用DVD。編排由淺入深，按級提升，只要讀者堅持學習，必能有效提高英語溝通能力。

商務印書館(香港)有限公司

編輯部

使用説明

百科英語階梯閱讀分四級，共八本書，是彩色有影有聲書，每本有英語文章供閱讀，根據數據庫如 *Collins Cobuild The Bank of English*、*British National Corpus* 及 *BYU Corpus of American English* 選收常用字詞編寫，配彩色照片及一張video/audio 兩用DVD，結合閱讀、聆聽、視像三種學習方式。

讀者可使用本書：

 學習新詞彙，並透過延伸閱讀(Expansion Reading) 練習速讀技巧

 聆聽錄音提高聽力，模仿標準英語讀音

 看短片做練習，以提升綜合理解能力

Grammar Focus解釋語法重點，後附練習題，供讀者即時複習所學，書內其他練習題，有助讀者掌握學習技巧如 scanning, prediction, summarising, identifying the main idea

中英對照生詞表設於書後，既不影響讀者閱讀正文，又具備參考作用

Contents 目錄

出版說明
使用說明

The CD-ROM contains a video and full recording of the text
CD-ROM 包括短片和錄音

Words to Know

This story is set in Mongolia.
It happens near Ulan Bator,
the capital city of Mongolia.

A **The Parts of a Horse.** Look at the picture. Write the letter of the correct word next to each definition.

1. the part of a horse's body that sticks out from the back: _____
2. the flat part of the face, above the eyes and below the hair: _____
3. the piece of hair that falls forward between a horse's ears: _____
4. the long body parts used for running and walking: _____

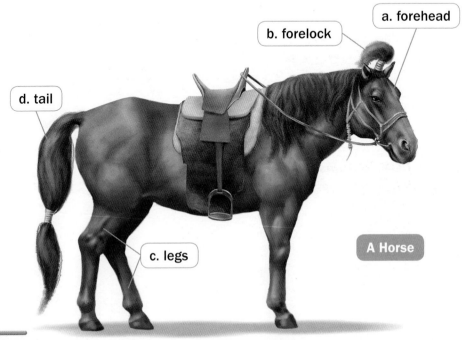

a. forehead
b. forelock
d. tail
c. legs
A Horse

B An Old Tradition. Read the paragraph. Then complete the sentences.

This story is about an interesting horse race in Mongolia. In the race, the riders make their horses run very fast, or gallop. The fastest horse and rider win the race. The race started in the 1200s, during the times of Genghis Khan. Genghis Khan was the emperor, or king, of a very big empire. Horses were very important in building his empire. He had a large cavalry with many excellent horsemen. Because of this, the sport of horse riding continues to be very important to many Mongolians today.

1. People from Mongolia are called M_____ .

2. When horses run very fast they g_____ .

3. An event to see who is the fastest is a r_____ .

4. An area ruled by one person is an e_____ .

5. The sport of riding horses is called h_____ r_____ .

6. The man who rules an empire is an e_____ .

7. A group of men who fight on horseback is a c_____ .

Genghis Khan
(c. 1162–1227)

A Horse and Rider

Mongolians are very good at horse riding. People all over the world think that they're great horsemen. It's something that has always been a part of Mongolian culture, even in the 1200s. In the days of the emperor Genghis Khan, Mongolia had a very strong cavalry. This cavalry helped the emperor to create one of the largest empires ever known.

Since the days of Genghis Khan, life on the quiet **steppes**[1] of Mongolia has changed. However, horses are still a very important part of the culture here. Many people often move from place to place. They need horses for their way of life, just as they did centuries ago.

---

[1]**steppe:** a large area of land with grass but no trees

Long ago, Mongolia had a very strong cavalry.

In Mongolia, people sometimes have events to show just how important horses are to them. Every year in July, thousands of people come from all over Mongolia to a place just outside the city of Ulan Bator. They come for the **festival**[1] of Naadam. This festival has several important traditional Mongolian sporting events – including horse riding. However, the Naadam race is a little unusual because the 'horsemen' at this event are just children. The riders must be younger than 12 years old!

---

[1] **festival:** special day with special activities

What do you think?

1. Are there any festivals in your country?

2. What events do they have?

3. Are there any special activities especially
   for young people?

On the day of the race, careful and detailed preparations begin early in the morning. The horses have to look very special. The racers cover each horse's tail with **leather**.[1] They also cover the **forelock**[2] on the horse's **forehead**.[3] Then, people offer horse's milk to the spirits of nature. Horse's milk has an important meaning in Mongolian culture. After that, they use **incense**[4] to clean the area around the rider of bad spirits. Finally, they put a drop of this milk near the legs to protect the rider and horse. At last, the horses and riders are ready for the big race.

---

[1] **leather:** animal skin often used to make shoes
[2] **forelock:** the front part of the long hair on a horse's neck
[3] **forehead:** the upper part of a horse's face
[4] **incense:** a substance that is burnt to produce a sweet smell

leather

Before the race, the young riders' parents join them to walk around a special area. It's an important day and the mothers and fathers want to see the race. Every parent hopes that their child will be one of the winners.

It's a big event – about 500 riders will **compete**[1] in the first race. It's a **demanding**[2] event as well; before the riders can even begin the race, they must walk the horses over 15 miles to the starting point.

---

[1] **compete:** try to win a race
[2] **demanding:** needing a lot of ability

Finally, the race begins. People wait at the finishing line to watch the race. However, they can't see anything at first. The race is so long that it's actually happening miles away. The horses and riders start far away and **gallop**[1] towards the finishing line.

The viewers want to get near the winning horses. An old story says that the **dust**[2] that rises into the air when the horses run is special. People believe that it brings happiness and success to anybody it touches.

---

[1] **gallop:** run at its fastest speed
[2] **dust:** small, dry pieces of earth

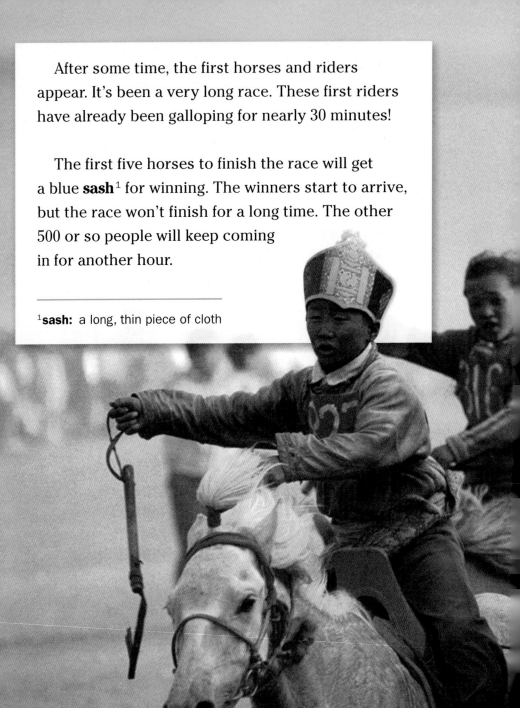

After some time, the first horses and riders appear. It's been a very long race. These first riders have already been galloping for nearly 30 minutes!

The first five horses to finish the race will get a blue **sash**[1] for winning. The winners start to arrive, but the race won't finish for a long time. The other 500 or so people will keep coming in for another hour.

---

[1]**sash:** a long, thin piece of cloth

Identify the Main Ideas

Skim the story. Find three unusual things about the race at the festival of Naadam. Make a list.

medal

sash

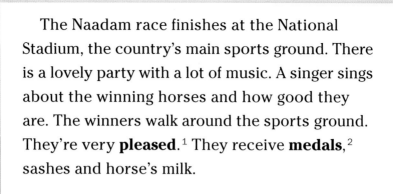

The Naadam race finishes at the National Stadium, the country's main sports ground. There is a lovely party with a lot of music. A singer sings about the winning horses and how good they are. The winners walk around the sports ground. They're very **pleased**.[1] They receive **medals**,[2] sashes and horse's milk.

---

[1] **pleased:** happy
[2] **medal:** a special circle of metal given to winners of a race

singer

It's the end of the Naadam race for another year. The race is very demanding for everyone involved. Indeed, these young riders are not just normal children. They have shown their **skills**[1] in one of Mongolia's most important traditions. They've shown that they may just be the next great riders in Mongolia!

---

[1] **skill:** ability to do an activity or job well

After You Read

1. Mongolians think that people all over the world are good at horse riding.
   A. True
   B. False

2. Today in Mongolia, _____ has changed since the days of Genghis Khan.
   A. not much
   B. a lot
   C. nothing
   D. everything

3. What is unusual about the riders in the Naadam race?
   A. They are good at horse riding.
   B. They are Mongolian.
   C. They are women.
   D. They are children.

4. When is the Naadam festival every year?
   A. January
   B. April
   C. July
   D. October

5. Which of the following is part of preparing a horse for the Naadam race?
   A. Cleaning the horse.
   B. Covering the forelock in leather.
   C. Changing the colour of the tail.
   D. Offering milk to the horses.

6. On page 13, the word 'begins' can be replaced by:
   A. starts
   B. does
   C. prepares
   D. joins

7. On page 14, who keep 'coming in for another hour'?
   A. children
   B. horses
   C. children and their horses
   D. parents

8. Mongolians believe the dust that the horses kick up is special.
   A. True
   B. False
   C. Doesn't say

9. What is a good heading for page 14?
   A. The First Riders Appear Quickly
   B. Galloping for 40 Minutes
   C. First Five Horses Get Blue Sash
   D. Winners Come After One Hour

10. In the story, how do the young winners feel after the race?
   A. lost
   B. pleased
   C. young
   D. energetic

11. What is the purpose of this story?
   A. To show the history of Mongolia.
   B. To show how to prepare for a horse race.
   C. To explain how to win a horse race.
   D. To show a great Mongolian tradition.

Genghis Khan

Genghis Khan was born in about 1165 in what is now called Mongolia. His life was not an easy one. His father was killed when Genghis was only nine years old. He then became responsible for his family. His mother taught him how to protect the family. This education was useful when he governed the empire that he created in later life. Genghis Khan was one of history's strongest leaders. He was responsible for bringing the Mongolian people together into a single nation. He achieved this by the time he was 30 years old.

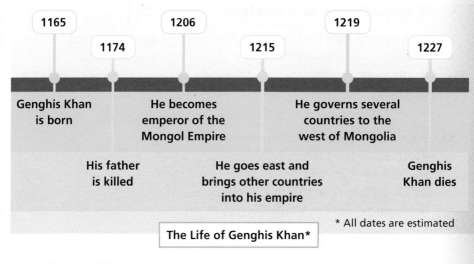

1165 — Genghis Khan is born

1174 — His father is killed

1206 — He becomes emperor of the Mongol Empire

1215 — He goes east and brings other countries into his empire

1219 — He governs several countries to the west of Mongolia

1227 — Genghis Khan dies

* All dates are estimated

The Life of Genghis Khan*

Genghis Khan learnt to ride a horse at a very young age and he taught his men how to ride as well. Their horse riding skills are well-known. His cavalry was one of the strongest and most fearless in the world. With the help of these men, this emperor changed Asia and the Middle East.

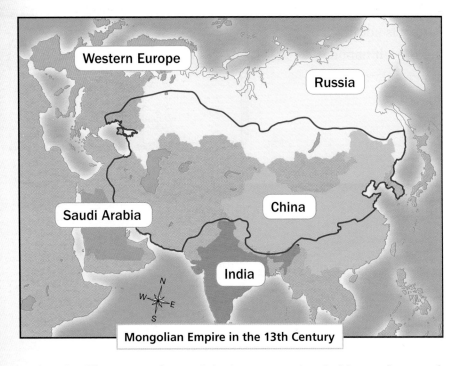

Mongolian Empire in the 13th Century

Genghis Khan created one of the largest empires in history. It started in Korea in the east and went all the way to Western Europe. During the Mongolian Wars, he and his cavalry moved across Asia and the Middle East. Khan then added each new country they entered to his empire. At one point, Khan's empire included parts of the countries we call China, Korea, Russia, and Mongolia.

Genghis Khan also achieved many other things. He set up the first trade agreements between the countries of Asia and the Middle East. He supported arts like painting. He even established a handwriting system for the Mongolian language. Over time, this led to increased trade and learning. To some people, Genghis Khan was only a strong fighter, to others he was a lot more.

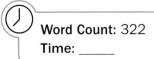

Word Count: 322
Time: _____

Words to Know

This story is set in South Korea. It happens in a place called Cheju Island.

SOUTH KOREA

Cheju Island

ASIA

SOUTH KOREA

N W E S

A **Scuba Divers.** Label the picture with the <u>underlined</u> words in the paragraph.

Divers are people who go underwater for enjoyment or their job. <u>Scuba divers</u> use an <u>oxygen tank</u>. It allows them to breathe underwater. Sometimes divers go into the <u>sea</u> to find <u>seafood</u>. Octopus, abalone, and sea urchin are common seafoods.

3. _____

2. _____

1. _____

octopus

4. _____

sea urchin

abalone

B **Cheju Divers.** Read the paragraph. Then match each word with the correct definition.

Cheju is a small island that is known for its legendary women divers. It's also a society that is changing. In the past, women in Cheju often had to become divers, or *haenyos*, to get money. It was dangerous, but there was no other way to make a living. Recently, more tourists have been coming to the island. The young women of Cheju now have more job choices. This story is about the differences between these two generations of women. It's about a young tour guide and her 63-year-old aunt, who is one of the last of the Cheju divers.

1. legendary _____	**a.** a visitor who travels for enjoyment
2. make a living _____	**b.** people of a similar age within a society or family
3. tourist _____	**c.** the sister of someone's father or mother
4. choice _____	**d.** possibility to pick one option out of many
5. generation _____	**e.** famous; having been around for a long time
6. tour guide _____	**f.** earn money for shelter, food, and other necessities
7. aunt _____	**g.** a person who shows visitors around and gives information about a place

A Cheju Diver

The island of Cheju off the coast of South Korea is known for its natural beauty. It's also known for its **volcanoes**,[1] which are no longer active. However, Cheju is also famous for something a little more unusual. It's famous for a group of **legendary**[2] women divers called *haenyos*.

These women dive into the sea every day to look for seafood. It's their job, and it's difficult and very dangerous work. They make these dives without oxygen **tanks**.[3] They can **hold their breath**[4] and stay underwater for up to five minutes.

---

[1]**volcano:** a mountain with a hole in the top
[2]**legendary:** famous for a long time
[3]**tank:** a large metal container
[4]**hold (one's) breath:** not take extra air into the body; keep air in the lungs

26

For hundreds of years, the women of Cheju Island have made their living from deep within the sea. They dive into the cold waters and catch **octopus**,[1] **abalone**,[2] and **sea urchins**.[3] The seafood they catch has fed the people of Cheju for a very long time. However, the present **generation**[4] of women divers on Cheju may be the last one. Things on this small island are starting to change.

---

[1] **octopus:** a sea animal with eight long arms
[2] **abalone:** a shellfish
[3] **sea urchin:** a sea animal which has a hard shell with sharp points
[4] **generation:** a particular group existing at a particular time

Sunny Hong is part of a new generation of Cheju women. She's a tour guide. Her life doesn't **depend on**[1] catching seafood from the sea. It depends on the tourists that have started visiting the island.

Sunny thinks that the job is just right for her. She says, 'I wanted to find some kind of job [in] which I can use my English, and also this kind of job fit[s] my **aptitude**.'[2]

---

[1]**depend on:** need sth to survive
[2] **aptitude:** *(unusual use)* natural ability or skill

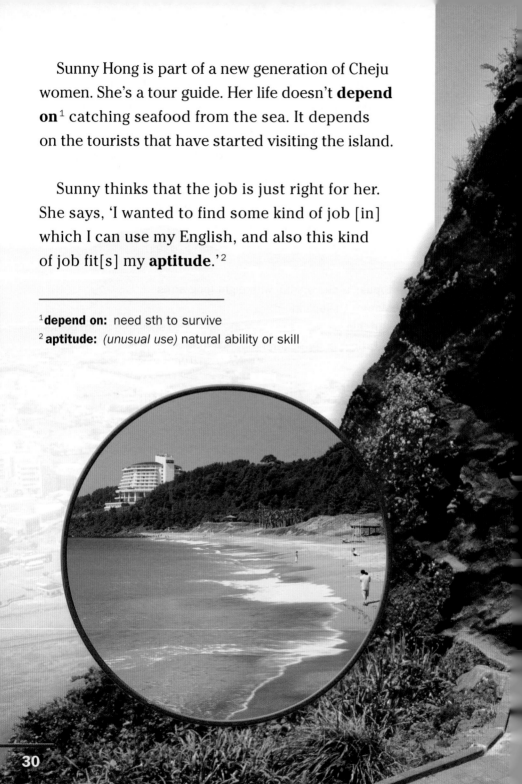

Sunny has taught herself English. It is this skill that has made her successful on land rather than having to depend on the sea. Until now, all of her female family members have worked in the sea as divers.

Sunny introduces her aunt, Ho Hong. 'This is my aunt, Ms. Hong. She's 63 years old and she started diving when she was thirteen,' Sunny explains, 'so [she has been diving for] almost fifty years now.' Sunny's aunt and her diver friends have been diving nearly all of their lives.

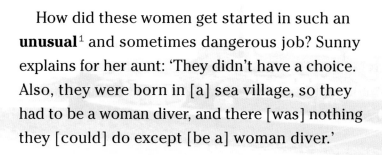

How did these women get started in such an
unusual[1] and sometimes dangerous job? Sunny
explains for her aunt: 'They didn't have a choice.
Also, they were born in [a] sea village, so they
had to be a woman diver, and there [was] nothing
they [could] do except [be a] woman diver.'

It's clear why the women didn't always choose
to be divers. The job is very dangerous. In fact, it's
the most dangerous job on the island, and it's only
done by women. But what makes it so dangerous?

---

[1]**unusual:** not common

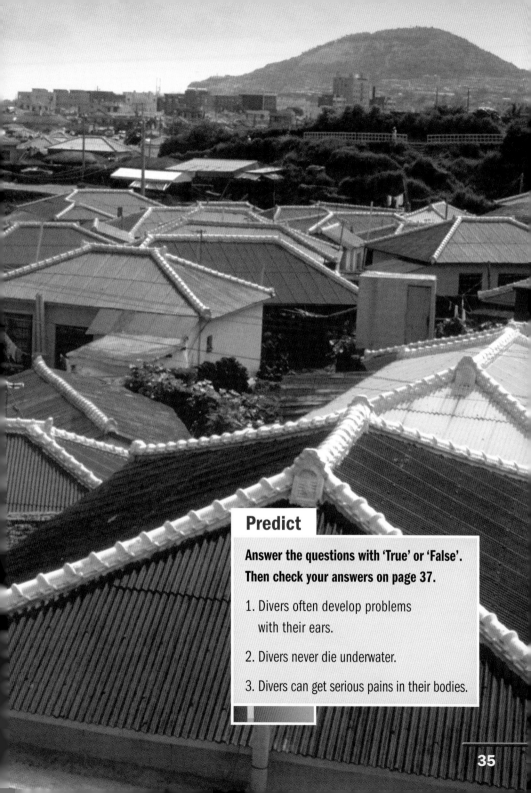

Predict

Answer the questions with 'True' or 'False'.
Then check your answers on page 37.

1. Divers often develop problems
   with their ears.

2. Divers never die underwater.

3. Divers can get serious pains in their bodies.

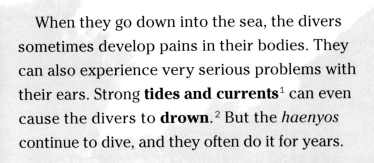

When they go down into the sea, the divers sometimes develop pains in their bodies. They can also experience very serious problems with their ears. Strong **tides and currents**[1] can even cause the divers to **drown**.[2] But the *haenyos* continue to dive, and they often do it for years.

This last generation of women divers is not a young one. The youngest diver on the island is 45 years old. The oldest diver is 75. These women dive for five to six hours every day. But why do they keep diving for so long?

---

[1]**tides and currents:** movements of the sea or ocean
[2]**drown:** die because of being unable to take in air while underwater

The answer is easy to understand when you look at the seafood they catch. 60-year-old Song Ho has had a good day. The seafood she has caught may make up to 300 U.S. dollars.

Diving is still a big business in Cheju and divers can **make a good living**[1] doing it. It used to be the only way the women could get food for their families. However, it now also gives them a chance to educate their children for a better life. So what about the next generation? What about the younger women of Cheju?

---

[1]**make a good living:** earn enough money to pay for everything you need

Divers can make up to 300 U.S. dollars on a good day.

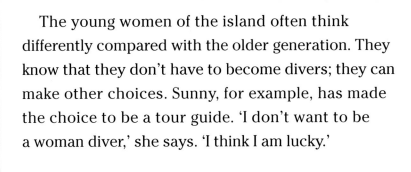

The young women of the island often think differently compared with the older generation. They know that they don't have to become divers; they can make other choices. Sunny, for example, has made the choice to be a tour guide. 'I don't want to be a woman diver,' she says. 'I think I am lucky.'

These choices may be making life better for the younger generation of Cheju. However, the very old tradition of the *haenyo* may be **dying out**.[1] Sunny's aunt and her friends may just be the last of the Cheju women divers.

---

[1]**die out:** not exist anymore

What do you think?

1. Do you think that Sunny is lucky?

2. Would you like to be a diver? Why or why not?

After You Read

1. Women divers _____ the island of Cheju dive into the sea every day.
   A. under
   B. from
   C. for
   D. into

2. Some people like to climb the volcanoes on the island of Cheju.
   A. True
   B. False
   C. Not in text

3. On page 29, 'they' in 'they catch' refers to:
   A. octopus, abalone, and sea urchin
   B. every woman in Cheju
   C. the men of Cheju
   D. divers on the island

4. Why is Sunny Hong part of a new generation?
   A. She wants to be an English teacher.
   B. She has chosen a different life.
   C. She has an aptitude for diving.
   D. all of the above

5. Learning to speak English has helped Sunny to:
   A. find a different job.
   B. depend on the sea.
   C. be like her aunt.
   D. dive for many years.

6. On page 33, what does 'depend on' mean?
   A. want
   B. have
   C. need
   D. take

7. Choose the best heading for page 34:

    A. Women Choose to Be Divers

    B. Diving Safest Job on Island

    C. Men Choose Dangerous Job

    D. Diving Is Only Option

8. Diving can be dangerous for people's ears.

    A. True

    B. False

9. On page 37, 'it' in the first paragraph refers to:

    A. developing pains

    B. diving

    C. experiencing problems

    D. drowning

10. What does Song Ho probably think about diving?

    A. Diving is an easy way to make a living.

    B. You can make a lot of money diving.

    C. Tour guides make more money.

    D. all of the above

11. How do women divers better educate their children?

    A. They teach them a lot about diving.

    B. They show them how to sell seafood.

    C. They teach them how wonderful diving is.

    D. They give them money to study.

12. Sunny thinks she is lucky _____ she can make other choices.

    A. why

    B. for

    C. because

    D. where

A Diving Holiday!

Are you looking for a different kind of holiday?

Every year thousands of tourists visit Hawaii. Many of them stay in hotels on the Big Island. Others make a different choice. Here at Hawaii Holidays, we offer activity holidays in Hawaii that are away from the majority of the tourists. We offer scuba diving holidays around this beautiful island. Our customers spend their holidays wearing oxygen tanks and diving deep into the sea. They do this in order to look at beautiful fish and unusual plants. There are many diving sites in the Hawaiian Islands. One of the most special is Lanai Lookout on the island of O'ahu.

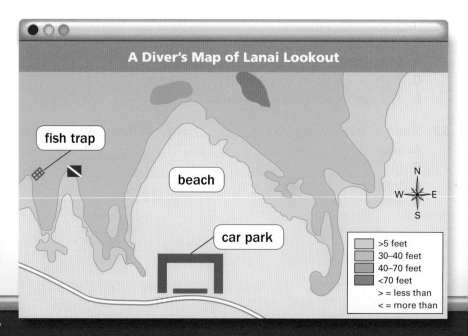

A Diver's Map of Lanai Lookout

fish trap

beach

car park

	>5 feet
	30–40 feet
	40–70 feet
	<70 feet
	> = less than
	< = more than

A view from Lanai Lookout

Why should you visit O'ahu with Hawaii Holidays?

O'ahu is 150 miles north of the Big Island of Hawaii. It is home to Hawaii's biggest city, Honolulu. Our customers usually stay in Honolulu. We take them to visit the most attractive places where they can enjoy nature. Lanai Lookout is a favourite place for divers who want to experience the beauty of this island. We offer a special scuba diving visit to Lanai Lookout.

A Day at Lanai Lookout

Beginner divers are not allowed to dive here. We only take experienced divers because the sea has very strong tides and currents. It can be dangerous for a beginner. Our visit to Lanai is an unforgettable experience. You begin by walking from the car park down to the sea. Before starting your dive, our trainers will help you to check the map to see how deep the water is. Your first stop is the well-known fish trap. This is where Hawaii University catches fish for scientific studies. During the dive, our trainers will help you to stay safe. They will ensure that you stay in areas where the water is less than 40 feet deep. We promise you will love the beauty of Lanai Lookout and enjoy this special dive.

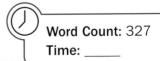

Word Count: 327
Time: _____

Words to Know

This story is set in the United States (U.S.), in the state of Hawaii. In the story, you will read about the city of Hilo.

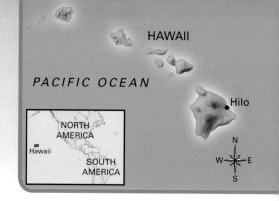

HAWAII

PACIFIC OCEAN

Hilo

NORTH AMERICA

Hawaii

SOUTH AMERICA

 A **The Hawaiian Islands.** Read the paragraph. Then match each word with the correct definition.

Hawaii is a group of islands in the Pacific Ocean. The islands are in a tropical area, which means that it is very hot there. Hawaii has the sea all around it, so it has many beautiful beaches. It is also a land with an ancient history and culture. Long ago, Hawaii had kings and queens that ruled the island. They were very powerful leaders. There are many legends in Hawaii as well. They tell interesting stories about the past.

1. island _____

2. sea _____

3. tropical _____

4. beach _____

5. ancient _____

6. queen _____

7. legend _____

a. a woman ruler

b. very old

c. a large body of water

d. an old story from the past

e. an area of sand or stones next to the sea

f. from or in the hottest parts of the world

g. an area of land that has water all around it

B **Hula Dancers.** Read the sentences. Then complete the paragraph with the underlined words.

The hula is a type of dance.
A *halau* is a school where they teach the hula.
Hula dancers wear special costumes.
Hawaiian people dance the hula at special events called festivals.
Spiritual means with strong feelings or beliefs.

In Hawaii, the hula is a very important traditional (1) _____. It's more than three hundred years old. Nowadays, Hawaiians dance the hula at (2) _____. For some, the hula is a (3) _____ dance that they relate to personal beliefs and feelings. People can learn the hula at a (4) _____. Most hula dancers wear beautiful (5) _____ and put flowers in their hair.

A Tropical Island

Hawaiian Hula Dancers

Hawaii is a truly beautiful place. Most people know Hawaii for its lovely beaches and its warm sea. However, Hawaii is also a land full of **legends**.[1] Several old stories have existed for many years on these **tropical**[2] islands. One of the oldest legends tell of a special dance called the hula, which started here more than three hundred years ago.

---

[1]**legend:** old story
[2]**tropical:** describing the hot part of the world near the equator

One hula teacher tells the story of how the dance started. 'The hula started, as far as legend tells it, when Hi'iaki and her good friend Hopoe went down to the beach. And then, when they were there, they noticed the waves … and they **imitated** [1] the waves. And then they started to use their hands … like **portraying** [2] the waves. That's how the hula started.'

_____

[1] **imitate:** behave in a similar way as sb or sth else
[2] **portray:** show; act like

sea

waves

beach

Sequence the Events

**What is the correct order of the events?
Read page 53, then number 1 to 4.**

_____ The queen banned the hula.

_____ The religious people were surprised.

_____ Dancers performed the hula
in secret.

_____ Religious people came to Hawaii.

However, not everyone has always liked the hula. In 1820, very **religious**[1] people from Western countries came to Hawaii. They were surprised by the hula because the dancers were not wearing many clothes. The visitors were so surprised, that they asked the queen of Hawaii to **ban**[2] the dance.

After that, Hawaiians were not allowed to perform the hula in public for almost sixty years. But that did not mean the dancing stopped. Many dancers still performed the hula **in secret**.[3] The dance was always there.

---

[1] **religious:** believing in God or gods
[2] **ban:** not allow; stop
[3] **in secret:** not seen or known about by most people

Years later, things have changed. At the moment, there is a **renewed**[1] interest in Hawaiian culture throughout these islands. People of all ages want to study the **ancient**[2] culture. They want to learn how to dance the hula.

This interest has resulted in an increase in the demand for hula lessons. So, more and more people are **attending**[3] *halaus. Halaus* are special schools that teach the hula in the traditional way. These schools also teach the traditional values and **discipline**[4] that go along with the dance.

---

[1]**renewed:** happening again after sth has stopped
[2]**ancient:** very old
[3]**attend:** go regularly to a place
[4]**discipline:** rules and control

The hula isn't an easy dance to do. First, the dancers must work very hard to learn it. Then, they have to practise for many hours. If they want to perform the dance for other people, they must be ready and well prepared.

One person who can help dancers prepare is Kumano Palini Kulala. Kumano is a hula teacher. For him, the dance is a way to **bring the best of**[1] ancient Hawaiian culture to people today.

---

[1]**bring the best of sth to sb:** find out the most attractive things and show them to sb

Kumano says that the dance is not really about the body. He feels that it's more about the mind. He also believes that it's a very spiritual dance. He explains his feelings: '... the hula is more ... not so much a **physical**[1] thing, but more of a **mental**[2] and a spiritual thing. For [new dancers], the dancing means very little, because for Hawaiians today, many of them don't speak the [Hawaiian] language. So, what I try to do is to bring to mind the reality that they see today.'

[1]**physical:** of the body
[2]**mental:** of the mind

Fact Check: True or false?

1. Dancers have to practise a lot.

2. Kumano Palini Kulala is a hula teacher.

3. The hula is only a physical thing.

4. Many Hawaiians don't speak the
   Hawaiian language.

With the help of people like Kumano, the hula has become an important part of Hawaiian life and culture once again. Because of this, there are now many hula festivals in Hawaii. Every year, the most important hula **competition**[1] happens in the city of Hilo. Dancers from all of the Hawaiian Islands come together at this festival. The festival is held in the name of a legendary Hawaiian king. This king helped to return the ancient hula dance to its place at the centre of Hawaiian culture.

In the competition, of course the **judges**[2] look at the way the dancers dance. But they look at more than just that. They also look at the dancers' **costumes**[3] and their style. The way the person wears a skirt, the colour of his or her costume, and the flowers they wear are all very important.

---

[1]**competition:** an event in which people try to be the best and win
[2]**judge:** someone who decides which person or thing wins
[3]**costume:** the clothing worn by a dancer

flowers

skirt

judges

Today in Hawaii, the ancient hula dance is **definitely**[1] not done in secret; it's a part of everyday life. It's once again a tradition that people can practise and perform often. It's a tradition that they can see at various festivals. And hopefully, it's a tradition that will continue for years and years to come.

---

[1]**definitely:** without any doubt

After You Read

1. The hula was created _____ three hundred years ago.
   A. more than
   B. exactly
   C. over
   D. less than

2. Which is a good heading for page 50?
   A. Two Girls Watch the Sea and Make a New Dance
   B. Teacher Creates Ancient Hula Story
   C. Legend of Hula Dance Began in the Sea
   D. Sea Imitated Hula

3. The religious visitors in 1820 probably came from:
   A. Hawaii.
   B. Asia.
   C. Europe and the U.S.
   D. Hilo.

4. What did the hula dancers do after the queen banned the dance?
   A. They stopped dancing.
   B. They danced in secret.
   C. They started wearing more clothes.
   D. They performed for everyone.

5. On page 53, 'they' in the first paragraph refers to:
   A. hula dancers
   B. the queen
   C. Hawaiians
   D. the visitors

6. The writer thinks that learning the hula is:
   A. easy work.
   B. simple work.
   C. difficult work.
   D. surprising work.

7. Kumano believes that the body is the most important part of hula.
   A. True
   B. False

8. What happens in Hilo every year?
   A. a big dance event
   B. a competition with judges
   C. a festival for a legendary king
   D. all of the above

9. On page 60, the word 'return' in the first paragraph means:
   A. bring back
   B. continue
   C. go home
   D. organise

10. In the competition, the judges look for more than _____ a person dances.
   A. which
   B. how
   C. who
   D. when

11. What is the purpose of this story?
   A. to show tradition is important
   B. to celebrate a great Queen
   C. to teach people how to dance the hula
   D. to show that competitions are easy

TRAVEL News

CARNIVAL IN TRINIDAD

Carnival in Trinidad is one of the longest and happiest parties you could possibly attend. It starts in December and goes on until February. Every year people from all over the world come to this festival. They come to enjoy the great music and unusual food. If you decide to visit Trinidad, you may also have the chance to join the party on this beautiful tropical island.

Kings and Queens Costume Competition

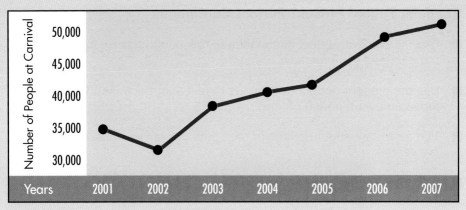

Rising Attendance at Carnival in Trinidad

The main events happen at the end of Carnival. One of the most interesting events is the 'Kings and Queens Costume Competition'. All of the musical groups from the Carnival have their own king and queen. This couple then appears in costume with their musical group. The costumes cost hundreds of U.S. dollars and take many months to create. Some of them are over thirty feet high! Every year, judges choose the best costumes.

In the beginning, Carnival had a religious purpose and the local churches organised the events. However, the people of Trinidad and Tobago originally came from many different cultures. Because of this, they soon began to incorporate other traditions. These traditions came from different parts of the world including South America, Africa, England, France, and India.

This makes Carnival one of the most colourful and varied festivals in the world. It also explains why people from so many different countries choose to attend Carnival.

The latest data shows that attendance at Carnival has risen almost every year since 2001. The figures show an increase from around 35,000 people in 2001 to over 50,000 in 2007. Six out of ten visitors to the country come from the United States, Canada, or the United Kingdom. Carnival attracts many people between December and February, but the island's beautiful beaches and sea bring thousands more visitors all year round.

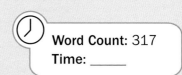

Word Count: 317
Time: _____

Grammar Focus: Present Perfect Continuous

■ Use the present perfect continuous to talk about actions that started in the past and continue now.

■ Use the present perfect continuous to talk about actions that are repeated over a period of time.

■ Use *for* to talk about periods of past time: *for ten minutes/one month/ five years.*

■ Use *since* to talk about a point in past time: *since 9:00/Wednesday/ 2004.*

I You They	have (not)		playing tennis waiting	since 3:00. for three hours.
		been	living here	since 2002.
Bill She	has (not)		studying working here	for a week. for six years.

Grammar Practice: Present Perfect Continuous

A. Write true sentences with the present perfect continuous and *for* or *since*.

e.g. I/live in this city   *I've been living in this city since 2001.*

1. we/learn English   _____
2. I/attend this school   _____
3. Mongolians/ride horse _____
4. I/do this worksheet   _____

B. Think of reasons for these situations and write sentences with the present perfect continuous.

e.g. Lisa is crying.   *She has been watching a sad movie.*

1. The dog is very dirty.   _____
2. Mary's eyes are red.   _____
3. The kitchen smells very good. _____
4. The horses are hot and tired.   _____
5. Our teacher is smiling.   _____

Grammar Focus: Present Perfect Continuous

She's sixty-three years old and she started diving when she was thirteen, so she <u>has been diving</u> [for] almost fifty years now.

■ In the example from the reading, the word *for* is omitted from the time expression *(for) almost fifty years now*. Omitting *for* is common in informal spoken English.

I				
You	have		playing football	since 4:30.
They			waiting	for three hours.
		been	living here	since 2006.
Bill			studying	for a week.
She	has		working here	for six years.

Grammar Practice: Present Perfect Continuous

C. Write sentences using the prompts with the present perfect continuous and *for* or *since*. You may also omit the word *for* as in the example sentence.

e.g. I/eat seafood/my whole life
   I have been eating seafood (for) my whole life.

1. Yoko/study English/four years

   _____

2. Pedro and Rita/live in this city/last November

   _____

3. You/talk on the telephone/2:00 this afternoon

   _____

4. I/work at my parents' store/a long time

   _____

■ Review the formation of questions with the present perfect continuous.

	have	he		learning English?
How long		Carol	been	living here?
		they		playing football?
	has	we		waiting?

Grammar Practice: Present Perfect Continuous

D. Write questions with the present perfect continuous tense, and give your answers which should include *for* or *since*.

e.g. How long/you/think about women divers?
How long have you been thinking about women divers?
Sample answers: ***since*** *yesterday morning* OR ***(for)*** *about two hours.*

1. How long/you/sit in this room?

_____

_____

2. How long/you/study English?

_____

_____

3. How long/you/attend this school?

_____

_____

4. How long/you/wear those shoes?

_____

_____

Grammar Focus: Relative Clauses: 'that/which'

■ Relative clauses give information about a noun. Grammatically, they are dependent clauses and must be connected to independent clauses.

■ *That* and *which* are relative pronouns. They connect relative clauses to independent clauses and can play the grammatical role of subject in relative clauses.

■ Restrictive relative clauses give information that is necessary to identify the noun in the main clause. In restrictive relative clauses, we use *that* to describe people or things and *which* to describe things.

■ Nonrestrictive relative clauses give additional information about the noun in the main clause. In nonrestrictive relative clauses, we always use the relative pronoun *which*, not *that*. Nonrestrictive clauses also can comment on or give more information about entire clauses.

■ Nonrestrictive relative clauses are always set off by commas.

My father is the person	that	taught me to read.
Education is something		will always be valuable.
This is a dish	which	my mother prepares very well.
My brother studied dance,		is why he dances so well.

Grammar Practice: Relative Clauses: 'that/which'

A. Fill in the blanks with *that* or *which*. In some sentences, both may be possible.

e.g. Mr. Kulala is the teacher ____*that*____ helped me learn hula dancing.

1. Hula is a dance _____ helps Hawaiians keep their cultural traditions.

2. I enjoy any kind of dancing, _____ is why I study hula dancing.

3. Please give this costume to someone _____ can use it.

4. I studied in a halau for two years, _____ is how I learned discipline.

B. Complete the sentences. Use your imagination!

e.g. Students like textbooks that *have a lot of examples.*_____

1. I like legends that _____

2. I never eat food that _____

3. _____, which is very expensive.

4. _____, which I was happy to do.

Video Practice

A. Watch the video of *The Young Riders of Mongolia* and choose the main idea.

1. Young people are continuing the traditional sport of horse riding in Mongolia.
2. The Naadam festival is the most important place to see Mongolian sports.
3. People in Mongolia think that the dust from horses brings happiness and success.

B. Watch Part 1 of the video again and circle the word you hear.

1. 'It's something that has (long/always) been a part of Mongolian culture.'
2. 'In the days of the emperor Genghis Khan, Mongolia had a very (large/strong) cavalry.'
3. 'However, horses are still an (big/important) part of the culture here.'
4. 'Each year in July, thousands of (visitors/people) come to a place just outside Ulan Bator.'
5. 'On the day of the first race, careful preparations (begin/start) early in the morning.'

C. Watch Part 2 of the video again and write the numbers.

1. 'It's a big event – about _____ riders will compete in the first race...'
2. '...first they must walk the horses over _____ miles to the starting point.'
3. 'These first riders have already been galloping for nearly _____ minutes!'
4. 'The first _____ horses to finish the race get a blue sash for winning.'
5. 'These young riders have shown their skills in _____ of Mongolia's most important traditions.'

D. Read the sentences. Watch the video of *The Last of the Cheju Divers* and circle True or False. Then correct the false sentences.

1. One woman diver catches an octopus.   True False
2. Sunny talks to her aunt, Ms. Hong, outside her house. True False
3. The woman divers sell their seafood outdoors.   True False

E. Read the sentences. Watch the video again and circle the word you hear.

   1. 'It's also known for something a little more unusual: a group of (legendary/famous) women divers called *haenyos*.'
   2. 'These women dive into the sea every day to look for (fish/seafood).'
   3. 'For hundreds of years, the women of Cheju have made their (money/living) from the sea.'
   4. 'However, the present generation of women divers on Cheju may be the (best/last).'
   5. 'Until now, all of her female family members have worked as (divers/swimmers).'

F. Read the questions. Watch the video again and answer the questions.

   1. Why did Sunny's aunt, Ms. Hong, become a woman diver?
   2. What is the most dangerous job on Cheju Island?
   3. What types of problems can divers have?
   4. How old is the youngest woman diver?
   5. Why do the women divers continue to dive?

G. Watch the video of *The Story of the Hula* and circle the word or words you hear.

   1. 'One of the oldest legends tells of a special dance called the hula, which started more than (two/three) hundred years ago.'
   2. 'They were (surprised/frightened) by the hula – the dancers did not wear many clothes!'
   3. 'After that, most Hawaiians were not allowed to (do/perform) the hula for almost sixty years.'
   4. 'But, dancers still performed the hula (inside/in secret).'

H. Watch the video again and complete the sentences.

   1. 'Hawaii is a land of _____.'
   2. 'These old stories have existed for many years on these beautiful tropical _____.'
   3. 'The visitors were so surprised, that they asked the _____ of Hawaii to ban the dance.'
   4. '... the hula is more ... not so much a physical thing, but more of a mental and a _____ thing.'

(1) The festival of Naadam has several different sporting events, including horse racing. **(2)** People of all ages can be a part of the festival's events. **(3)** However, there is a special horse race for children ages 12 and under. **(4)** About 500 children ride in this race each year. **(5)** Before they can begin, they must walk the horses over 15 miles to the starting point. **(6)** Lots of people wait at the finish line to watch the race. **(7)** There is a lot of dust in the air. **(8)** After about 30 minutes, the first horses appear. **(9)** The first five horses that cross the finish line get a blue sash. **(10)** The winning riders get medals and horse's milk. **(11)** At the end, a singer sings about the winning horses and how good they are.

1. The first _____ horses to finish the race get a blue sash.
   A. five
   B. twelve
   C. fifteen
   D. thirty

2. Where should this sentence go? Some people think the dust brings happiness to anybody it touches.
   A. after sentence 1
   B. after sentence 3
   C. after sentence 5
   D. after sentence 7

3. The word 'they' in sentence 5 refers to _____.
   A. horses
   B. riders
   C. sporting events
   D. festivals

4. The best heading for this paragraph is _____,
   A. The Children of Mongolia
   B. The Festival of Naadam
   C. How to Win a Horse Race
   D. Horse Racing at Naadam

5. Which of the following describes the special horse race at the festival of Naadam?
   A. The riders are under 12 years old.
   B. Eight hundred people ride in it.
   C. All the horses finish in 30 minutes.
   D. The riders ride their horses to the starting point.

6. The winners of the horse race don't get _____.
A. medals
B. a blue sash
C. horse's milk
D. money

7. Mongolians _____ from place to place for thousands of years.
A. move
B. has been moved
C. have been moving
D. have moving

8. A young boy _____ for 30 minutes. He's almost at the finish line.
A. is riding
B. has been riding
C. riding
D. have been riding

9. An emperor is similar to a _____.
A. large city
B. race
C. king
D. horse

10. Horses use their _____ to walk and run.
A. forelocks
B. legs
C. tails
D. foreheads

(1) For many years, the women of Cheju Island in South Korea have made a living as divers. (2) Today these women divers can make as much as 300 U.S. dollars a day. (3) However, the job is dangerous and most younger women on the island don't want to do it. (4) Right now, the youngest diver is 45 years old and the oldest is 75. (5) In the past, diving was the only way women could get food for their families. (6) Now it helps them save money for their children's education. (7) However, today the younger women have other choices as well, which is a good thing. (8) For example, a young woman named Sunny Hong didn't want to become a woman diver. (9) She decided to become a tour guide instead. (10) She said that she wanted some kind of job that she would be good at and where she could use the English language.

11. In the past, the women of Cheju became divers because _____.
  A. they loved to dive
  B. they needed food for their families
  C. the job was interesting
  D. they didn't want to become tour guides

12. How old is the oldest diver on Cheju Island?
  A. 25
  B. 45
  C. 60
  D. 75

13. The writer thinks that _____.
  A. the young women don't like the older women
  B. the older women should not have been divers
  C. the younger women are more fortunate than the older ones
  D. more young women should become divers

14. What is the purpose of this paragraph?
  A. to show how life is changing on Cheju Island
  B. to encourage more young women to become divers
  C. to show the various jobs younger women are choosing
  D. to explain why older women continue to dive

15. The word 'it' in sentence 6 refers to _____.
  A. job
  B. food
  C. money
  D. diving

16. Nowadays, the women divers of Cheju _____.
  A. give the seafood they catch to their families
  B. are mostly older women
  C. make very little money
  D. become tour guides when they get older

17. The sister of someone's father or mother is _____.
   A. a diver
   B. an ocean
   C. a tourist
   D. an aunt

18. Something that can help people breathe under water is _____.
   A. a diver
   B. a generation
   C. an oxygen tank
   D. a choice

19. Decide which underlined word or phrase is incorrect.
   When Jim has been finishing
   A   B
   his homework he went to bed.
                        C
   He has been sleeping for twelve hours.   D

20. Yoko _____ to find a new job since March.
   A. has been trying
   B. have tried
   C. tries
   D. is trying

(1) Today there is a renewed interest in Hawaiian culture. (2) Many people want to learn how to dance the hula. (3) Hawaiians dance the hula at special events called festivals. (4) For some, doing the dance is a spiritual experience. (5) One teacher says that the dance is not about the body. (6) It's about the mind. (7) Every year there is a dance festival in Hilo, Hawaii. (8) Dancers from all the Hawaiian Islands dance at the festival. (9) The dancers wear special costumes. (10) There is a competition where judges look at the way each person dances. (11) The ancient hula dance is once again an important part of everyday life in Hawaii.

21. According to the paragraph, in Hawaii today, _____.
   A. no one does the hula
   B. there is a lot of interest in the hula
   C. there are no hula teachers
   D. Hawaiians only dance the hula at home

22. _____ dance at the hula festival every year.
   A. Dancers from all the Hawaiian Islands
   B. Only dancers from Hilo
   C. Dancers all over the world
   D. Only dance teachers

23. The best heading for this paragraph is _____.
   A. Hula Costumes
   B. How People Learn the Hula
   C. Hawaiian Festivals
   D. The Hula Today

24. Where should this sentence go? They also wear special flowers.
   A. after sentence 2
   B. after sentence 5
   C. after sentence 9
   D. after sentence 10

25. Which sentence is true?
   A. Everyone in Hawaii does the hula.
   B. Doing the hula is a spiritual experience for some dancers
   C. There are several important hula festivals in Hawaii each year.
   D. No dancers from Hilo dance in the festival.

26. The word 'some' in sentence 4 refers to _____.
   A. dancers
   B. teachers
   C. festivals
   D. judges

27. _____ is a word that
means 'an area of sand or stones
next to the sea.'
   A. Ocean
   B. Legend
   C. Tropical
   D. Beach

28. A 'halau' is _____.
   A. a hula festival
   B. a hula school
   C. a hula teacher
   D. a special kind of hula dance

29. Which sentence is correct?
   A. I found a school teaches hula
   dancing.
   B. I found a school that it teaches
   hula dancing.
   C. I found a school which teaches
   hula dancing.
   D. I found a school that they teach
   hula dancing.

30. Which sentence is correct?
   A. The hula is a dance that is very
   old.
   B. The hula is a dance is very old.
   C. The hula is a dance which it is very
   old.
   D. The hula that is a dance very old.

Key 答案

The Young Riders of Mongolia
Words to Know: A. 1. d **2.** a **3.** b **4.** c
B. 1. Mongolians **2.** gallop **3.** race **4.** empire **5.** horseback riding
6. emperor **7.** cavalry
What do you think?: open answers
Identify the Main Ideas: (suggested answers) The riders are all under 12 years old; they must walk 15 miles before the race; there are five winners.
After You Read: 1. B **2.** B **3.** D **4.** C **5.** B **6.** A **7.** C **8.** A **9.** C **10.** B **11.** D

The Last of the Cheju Divers
Words to Know: A. 1. sea **2.** diver **3.** oxygen tank **4.** seafood **B. 1.** e **2.** f **3.** a **4.** d **5.** b **6.** g **7.** c
Predict: 1. True **2.** False **3.** True
What do you think?: open answers
After You Read: 1. B **2.** C **3.** D **4.** B **5.** A **6.** C **7.** D **8.** A **9.** B **10.** B **11.** D **12.** C

The Story of the Hula
Words to Know: A. 1. g **2.** c **3.** f **4.** e **5.** b **6.** a **7.** d **B. 1.** dance **2.** festivals **3.** spiritual **4.** halau **5.** costumes
Sequence the Events: 3, 2, 4, 1
Fact Check: 1. True **2.** True **3.** False **4.** True
After You Read: 1. A **2.** A **3.** C **4.** B **5.** D **6.** C **7.** B **8.** D **9.** A **10.** B **11.** A

Grammar Practice

Present Perfect Continuous: A. (suggested answers) **1.** We have been learning English for three hours. **2.** I have been attending this school since 2002. **3.** Mongolians have been riding horses for centuries. **4.** I have been doing this worksheet since yesterday. **B.** (suggested answers) **1.** He has been playing in the mud. **2.** She has been crying. **3.** My mother has been cooking. **4.** They have been running. **5.** The students have been working hard. **C. 1.** Yoko has been studying English for four years. **2.** Pedro and Rita have been living in this city since last November. **3.** You have been talking on the telephone since 2:00 this afternoon. **4.** I have been working at my parents' store for a long time. **D. 1.** How long have you been sitting in this room? **2.** How long have you been studying English? **3.** How long have you been attending this school? **4.** How long have you been wearing those shoes?

Relative Clauses: 'that/which': A. 1. that/which **2.** which **3.** that **4.** which **B.** (suggested answers) **1.** have an unexpected ending. **2.** is difficult to digest. **3.** He has a rare book **4.** She asked me to perform a dance

Video Practice

A. 1. B. 1. always **2.** strong **3.** important **4.** people **5.** begin **C. 1.** 500 **2.** 15 **3.** 30 **4.** five **5.** one **D. 1.** True **2.** False **3.** True **E. 1.** legendary **2.** seafood **3.** living **4.** last **5.** divers **F. 1.** It was the only job she could do. **2.** being a diver **3.** body pain, ear problems, or even drowning **4.** 45 years old **5.** They can earn up to 300 U.S. dollars in a day. **G. 1.** three **2.** surprised **3.** perform **4.** in secret **H. 1.** legends **2.** islands **3.** queen **4.** spiritual

Exit Test

1. A **2.** D **3.** B **4.** D **5.** A **6.** D **7.** C **8.** B **9.** C **10.** B **11.** B **12.** D **13.** C **14.** A **15.** D **16.** B **17.** D **18.** C **19.** B **20.** A **21.** B **22.** A **23.** D **24.** C **25.** B **26.** A **27.** D **28.** B **29.** C **30.** A

English - Chinese Vocabulary List 中英對照生詞表

(Arranged in alphabetical order)

abalone	鮑魚	incense	焚香時的煙
ancient	古老	judge	裁判員
aptitude	天資	leather	皮革
attend	參加	legend	傳說
ban	被禁止	legendary	傳奇的
bring the best of sth to sb	呈現（某人／物）最佳的一面	make a good living	賺取很好的生活費
compete	競爭	medal	頒給勝出者的圓形金屬掛飾
competition	比賽	mental	精神的
costume	服裝	octopus	章魚
definitely	絕對的	physical	身體的
demanding	苛求的	pleased	高興的
depend on	倚靠	portray	扮演
discipline	紀律	religious	篤信宗教的
die out	逐漸消失	renewed	更新復興
drown	淹死	sash	飾帶
dust	塵埃	sea urchin	海膽
festival	節慶	skill	技巧
forehead	前額	steppe	大草原
forelock	馬鬃	tank	罐
gallop	奔馳	tides and currents	潮汐與海流
generation	一代；世代	tropical	熱帶的
hold (one's) breath	止住呼吸	unusual	不平常
imitate	模仿	volcano	火山
in secret	偷偷的		